THE WISDOM
— OF —
GRATITUDE

and a dozen ways to
contemplate and
express it

Atria
SENIOR LIVING

ENGAGE LIFE®

An important part of our promise
to our residents is to help them
continue to grow and enhance
their lives through the power of
connection, and to provide them with
opportunities for joy and fulfillment.

With *The Wisdom of Gratitude*,
we invite them to access their
enormous capacity for thankfulness
and see their lives grow richer
and more fulfilling in the process.
And through our signature
Engage Life program, we will
help our residents explore the
stories and exercises that follow.

FOR OUR DEAR RESIDENTS, WHO TEACH US
MORE ABOUT GRATITUDE EVERY SINGLE DAY
THAN WE COULD EVER PUT IN A SINGLE BOOK.

— YOUR ATRIA FAMILY

Contents

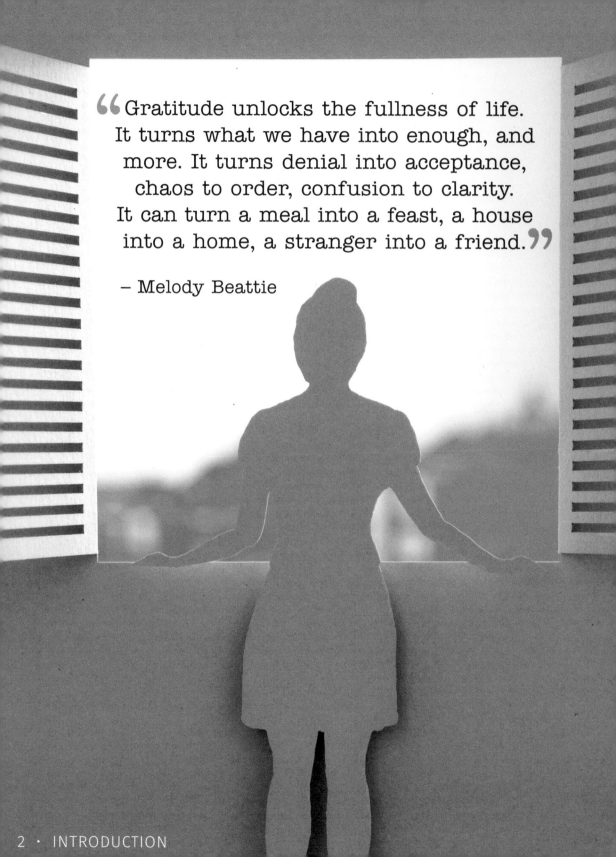

"Gratitude unlocks the fullness of life. It turns what we have into enough, and more. It turns denial into acceptance, chaos to order, confusion to clarity. It can turn a meal into a feast, a house into a home, a stranger into a friend."

– Melody Beattie

You have the power to be in the midst of the best, most fulfilling part of your life *right now*.

If you already feel that way, you are almost certainly in a place of gratitude. This book will help you continue to explore it.

If not, there could be many reasons why – pain, loss or simply being busy. But what you and every other human being have is the power to live in a state of gratitude – that means focusing on the goodness in what you do have instead of dwelling on what you don't.

Whether you realize it or not, the longer you've lived, the greater your capacity for thankfulness based on the sheer breadth of your life experience. You also have greater potential to reap the benefits of living in gratitude, as it can be a powerful antidote to whatever challenges you are facing.

Science describes gratitude as personality strength – the ability to be keenly aware of the good things that happen to you and never take them for granted. Grateful individuals express their thanks and appreciation to others in a heartfelt way, not just to be polite. If you possess a high level of gratitude, you often feel an emotional sense of wonder, thankfulness and appreciation for life itself – and researchers are finding that individuals who exhibit and express the most gratitude are happier and healthier.

No one can take gratitude away from you. It isn't dependent on a person, place or thing, nor is it dependent on how much you have or don't have. It's all in how you perceive it.

"**I WOULD MAINTAIN THAT THANKS ARE THE HIGHEST FORM OF THOUGHT, AND THAT GRATITUDE IS HAPPINESS DOUBLED BY WONDER.**"

– G.K. CHESTERTON

There are things we naturally and
spontaneously feel thankful for: our
family, the meal we are about to eat,
a kind gesture or a beautiful day.

This book presents you with the
opportunity to explore thankfulness
through a wider lens – that of the
wondrous, intangible qualities, ideals
and emotions that help define our
human experience. Things like resilience.
Perspective. Courage. Love.

Stories, essays and quotations will help
prime your brain – and your heart – for
meaningful consideration of each theme.
And thought-provoking exercises will
help you contemplate and express your
gratitude in ways that will enrich your life
(and quite likely the lives of others, too).

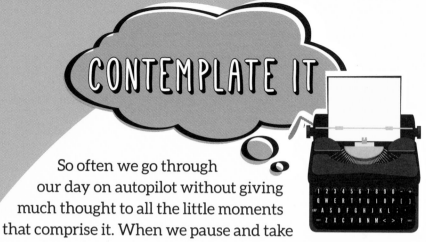

CONTEMPLATE IT

So often we go through our day on autopilot without giving much thought to all the little moments that comprise it. When we pause and take the time to be fully present to the wonder of our surroundings and fellow people, we are on a clear path to gratitude.

The "Contemplate It" exercises in each chapter invite you to put on your thinking cap, open your heart and observe all the people and things in your life in a more mindful way.

JOURNAL PAGES

Throughout your exploration of gratitude, you'll be invited (and hopefully inspired) to put certain things in writing. We've included plenty of space after each chapter for you to collect all your thankful thoughts.

POSTCARDS

Sending a heartfelt note is still the gold standard when it comes to expressing one's appreciation. We've included a unique assortment of postcards in your book's back pocket to help you spread the joy.

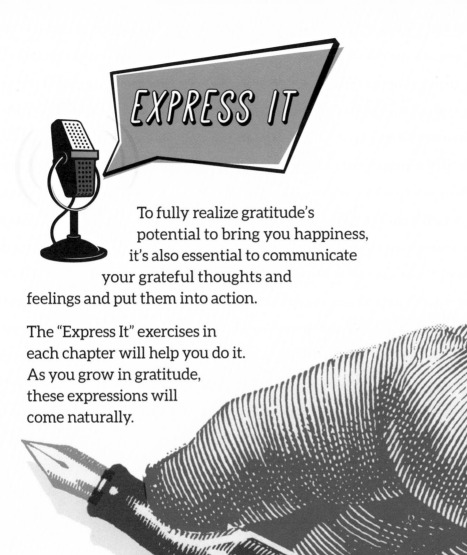

EXPRESS IT

To fully realize gratitude's potential to bring you happiness, it's also essential to communicate your grateful thoughts and feelings and put them into action.

The "Express It" exercises in each chapter will help you do it. As you grow in gratitude, these expressions will come naturally.

"Life is 10 percent what you make it and 90 percent how you take it."

– Irving Berlin

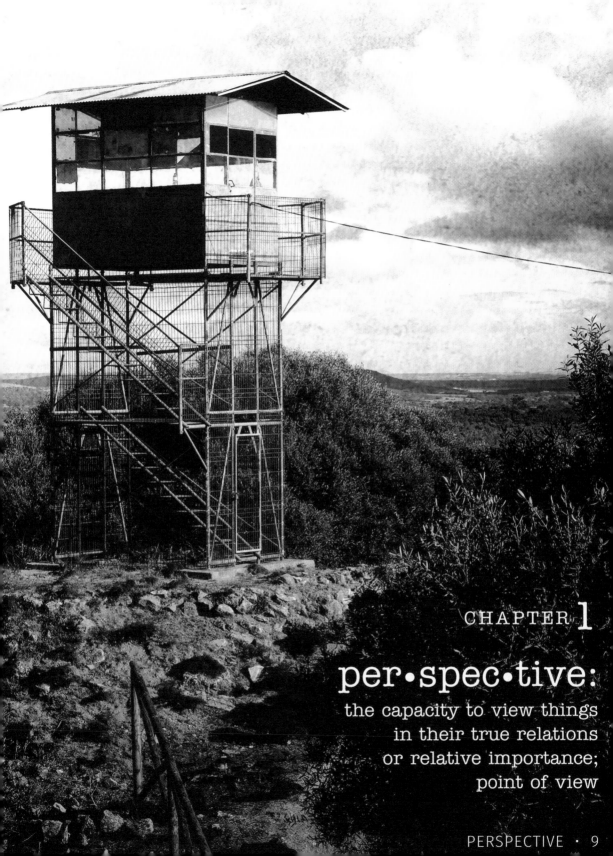

CHAPTER 1

per·spec·tive:
the capacity to view things
in their true relations
or relative importance;
point of view

THE OVERVIEW EFFECT

"ONCE A PHOTOGRAPH OF THE EARTH, TAKEN FROM OUTSIDE, IS AVAILABLE, A NEW IDEA AS POWERFUL AS ANY OTHER IN HISTORY WILL BE LET LOOSE."

English astronomer Fred Hoyle made this prediction in 1948. Whether or not he realized it at the time, Hoyle was foreshadowing a phenomenon astronauts would later experience when seeing Earth from space.

Writer and philosopher Frank White coins this phenomenon *the overview effect* in his like-titled 1987 book, which shares accounts of astronauts whose perspective on life was fundamentally changed after seeing the planet from hundreds of miles above.

From such a distance, national boundaries vanish. Wars and conflicts seem trivial. And Earth appears as a fragile ball hanging in the void, protected by only a paper-thin atmosphere.

Many reported a blissful feeling, becoming entranced and gazing at the Earth for hours on end. Apollo 14 astronaut Edgar Mitchell said peering at the Earth made him aware that every single atom in the universe was in some way connected, and that everyone and everything was bound together by a common cosmic existence.

Only about 500 people have been able to look back on the Earth from space. But you don't have to be an astronaut to understand how, sometimes, moving farther away from something can bring you closer to fully appreciating it.

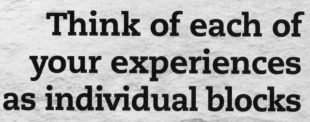

Think of each of your experiences as individual blocks

– the big important ones and the seemingly insignificant ones. Each new experience you have adds another block, building a stack that grows taller and stronger the more experiences you have.

Now picture yourself standing high atop your stack of blocks. From that lofty perch, you are able to look around and see all the people you can thank for your successes. All the people you can forgive for hurting you. The best in all that surrounds you. When you take it all in at the same time, you can really see what's most important and what doesn't matter.

The more years you've lived, the higher your stack of experiences, the better the view. And when you have so many blocks, you can spare a few for someone else who really needs them.

Reflect on a time when you were younger when something seemed so significant or dire – a test, a broken heart, a change.

If you knew then what you know now,

would it have seemed so... important?

Now think about how your younger self would have dealt with a situation you are facing today – an illness, a decision, a loss. Would you have handled it as well back then?

2

1 Think of someone who shared their perspective with you

and helped you see something in a different way that led you to a greater understanding. It could be the neighbor you discuss politics with, the caregiver from another country, the author of a newspaper editorial. Write and send them a thank-you note, and be sure to explain exactly why you are thanking them. They'll be glad to hear they made a difference.

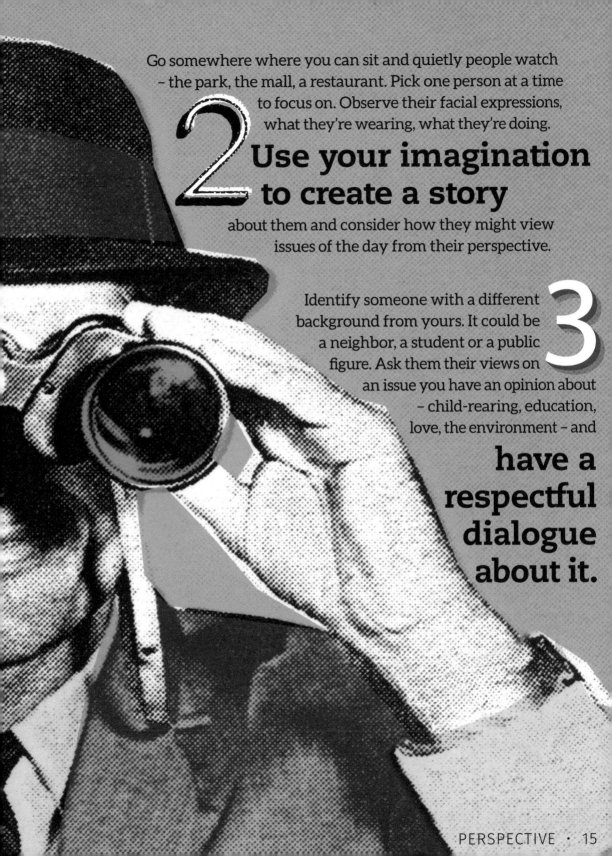

Go somewhere where you can sit and quietly people watch – the park, the mall, a restaurant. Pick one person at a time to focus on. Observe their facial expressions, what they're wearing, what they're doing.

2 Use your imagination to create a story

about them and consider how they might view issues of the day from their perspective.

Identify someone with a different background from yours. It could be a neighbor, a student or a public figure. Ask them their views on an issue you have an opinion about – child-rearing, education, love, the environment – and

3

have a respectful dialogue about it.

PERSPECTIVE: MY THANKFUL THOUGHTS

Date: _____

Date: _____

PERSPECTIVE: MY THANKFUL THOUGHTS

Date: _____

Date: _____

"BEING DEEPLY LOVED BY SOMEONE GIVES YOU STRENGTH, WHILE LOVING SOMEONE DEEPLY GIVES YOU COURAGE."

– LAO TZU

love:

a feeling of strong
or constant affection
for a person; warm
attachment, enthusiasm
or devotion to something;
unselfish, loyal and
benevolent concern
for the good of
another; a person's
adoration of God

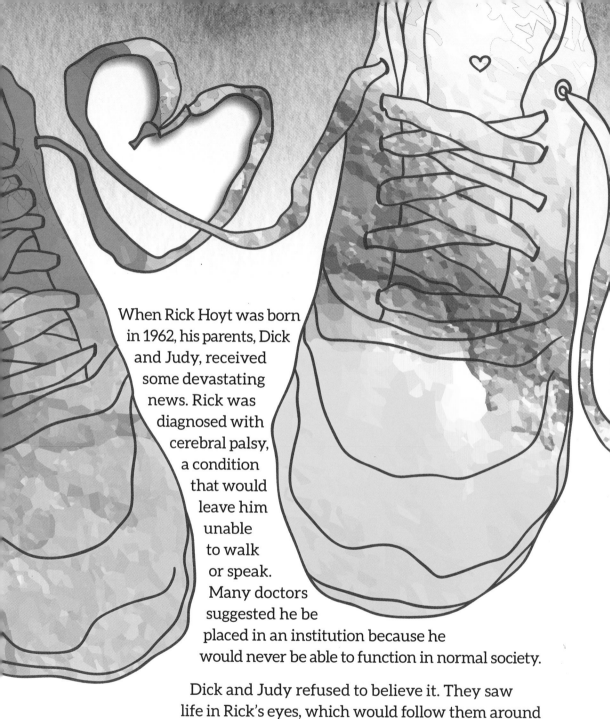

When Rick Hoyt was born in 1962, his parents, Dick and Judy, received some devastating news. Rick was diagnosed with cerebral palsy, a condition that would leave him unable to walk or speak. Many doctors suggested he be placed in an institution because he would never be able to function in normal society.

Dick and Judy refused to believe it. They saw life in Rick's eyes, which would follow them around the room. They sensed the spirit inside of him and held out hope he would someday be able to communicate with the outside world.

By the time Rick was 11 years old, technology was available that could help him communicate. He was fitted with a computer that allowed him to speak for the first time, and it soon became clear Rick was intelligent. With his new communication device, he was able to attend school.

In 1977 at the age of 15, Rick asked his father if they could run a five-mile race to benefit a lacrosse player who had become paralyzed. Dick, who was 36 at the time, was not a runner, but he agreed to race while pushing his son in a wheelchair. After the race, Rick typed out on his computer,

"Dad, when we run, it feels like my disability disappears."

That was all Dick needed to hear – "Team Hoyt" was born.

Since Rick was away at school and studying, Dick began training every day by pushing a 94-pound bag of cement in a wheelchair to simulate Rick's weight. The way Dick saw it, he was simply loaning his arms and legs to his son.

The two continued racing and as of April 2014, Team Hoyt had competed in more than 1,100 endurance events, including 72 marathons and six Ironman® triathlons. They have run the Boston Marathon® 32 times and biked across the United States, traveling 3,735 miles in 45 days.

In 2013, a statue of the Hoyts was dedicated near the start of the Boston Marathon in Hopkinton, Massachusetts. It serves as a symbol of hope, perseverance and the power of a father's unconditional love.

Love is precious and powerful – yet there is no limit to how much we can give or receive. In fact, it tends to grow exponentially and is highly contagious.

Make a list of everyone you have ever loved in your entire life

– family, a higher power, friends, sweethearts, pets. Beside that list, make a list of everyone who has ever loved you.

Consider how amazing it is to have the capacity for so much love in your heart.

Are your lists longer than you thought they would be when you started? How does it feel to see all those names together?

CONTEMPLATE IT

There are many ways to say "I love you." Think about all the ways – beyond words – you have shown your love to others. Spending time with them. Sending them a card or letter. Cutting the crusts off their sandwiches for lunch every day. Giving a thoughtful gift. Sharing hugs and kisses.

Think about all the different ways others have shown their love to you – the grand gestures and the simple acts. Making your favorite dinner. Moving to another city to be with you. Calling just to see how you're doing. Laughing at your jokes.

As you go about your day, **think of everything you do for others and everything they do for you as an expression of love.**

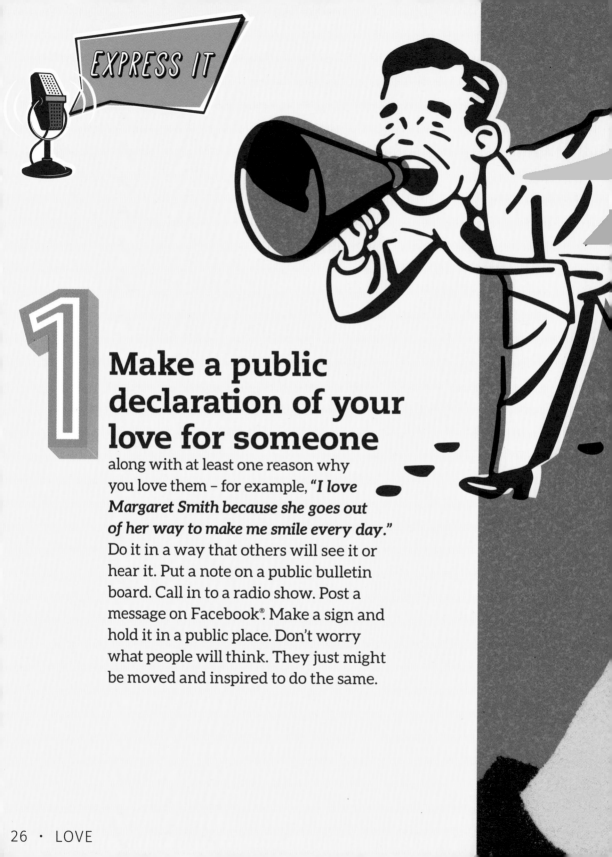

1

Make a public declaration of your love for someone

along with at least one reason why you love them – for example, *"I love Margaret Smith because she goes out of her way to make me smile every day."* Do it in a way that others will see it or hear it. Put a note on a public bulletin board. Call in to a radio show. Post a message on Facebook®. Make a sign and hold it in a public place. Don't worry what people will think. They just might be moved and inspired to do the same.

Write a love letter to love itself.

2

Recount the first time you experienced it. Describe the ways it has made you feel – good about yourself, warm, like you were floating on air, stomach in knots. Talk about how it guides your relationships with your family, your spouse, your friends and your faith. Explain how it helped you through hard times and forgive it for the times it betrayed you. Express as eloquently as you can your deep gratitude for the joy and meaning love has brought to your life.

LOVE: MY THANKFUL THOUGHTS

Date: _____

Date:

LOVE: MY THANKFUL THOUGHTS

Date: _____

Date:

"Everyone is born creative; everyone is given a box of crayons in kindergarten. Then when you hit puberty they take the crayons away and replace them with dry, uninspiring books on algebra, history, etc. Being suddenly hit years later with the 'creative bug' is just a wee voice telling you, 'I'd like my crayons back, please.'"

– Hugh MacLeod

cre•a•tiv•i•ty:

the ability to make new things or think of new ideas; the ability to use the imagination to develop new and original ideas or things; ingenuity

Fallas is a traditional celebration held in March in Valencia, Spain, in honor of Saint Joseph.

A five-day festival of art, light, noise and fire,

Fallas marks the end of winter and symbolizes the rejuvenation of the coming spring. Locals celebrate by building – and then burning – hundreds of elaborate monuments, donning traditional dress and participating in fireworks displays, parades, bullfights, religious processions, cooking competitions, concerts and dancing.

Each neighborhood has a *casal*, which is a club dedicated entirely to *Fallas*. For members of the *casal*, *Fallas* is a year-round cycle of meetings, competitions, fundraising parties and monument planning.

But nearly every resident of Valencia participates in the festival in some way, making it

a grand, collective and public expression of creativity

– not just that of a select few who have been deemed to be "artists."

1

Creativity is something that people tend to define in terms of art – painting, writing, dancing, singing and so on. But more often, creativity exists in everyday objects and actions, and it's created by normal human beings.

During the most ordinary actions of your day, thoughtfully consider the creativity that went into making them possible.

As you brush your teeth, look at your toothbrush. It's probably different from that of anyone else you know. Think of all the people who designed all those unique toothbrushes – different colors, special bristle strengths, various patterns and textures, custom sizes – just to appeal to our unique preferences. As you wash your hands, think of the people who were tired of dropping bar soap and found a better way – the pump dispenser. Go even farther and think about the people who figured out how to get the water from the reservoir all the way to your sink just so you can brush your teeth and wash your hands. What else can you discover the creativity in?

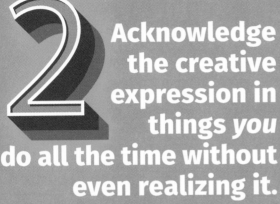

2

Acknowledge the creative expression in things *you* do all the time without even realizing it.

Throughout the day, be conscious of the thought and action involved in the clothes you choose or the way you style your hair. The way you figured out how to carry all your belongings as you walked out the door or the words you carefully selected that spared someone's feelings. If you're good at games, it's likely because you find creative ways to win. If you are good at fixing or repairing things, that's creative. Be grateful for your own talents and every opportunity you have to share them.

3

Actively appreciate public art and how it makes life more beautiful.

Sit and have lunch in a local park. Observe the architecture along the route on your next walk. Take a closer look at the sculptures in front of the courthouse or library.

EXPRESS IT

1 Attend a play, concert, art exhibit or craft show and thank the artist personally

for sharing their creativity – either in person, by letter or in an online review. Tell them about the pleasure or awe their work inspired in you.

2 Do something – anything – creative with the goal of delighting.

Do it with others or just by yourself. Write a poem. Bake a cake. Be a "human surprise" by showing up to cheer where someone least expects it. Make something with your hands. Sing a song. Consider what a gift it is to be able to please and inspire others.

Think of a song, painting, book, performance, poem or other "traditional" work of art that moves you deeply and you are grateful to have experienced. **Share it with someone else** – listen to a recording of it together, show them a picture of it, see it in person or loan them your copy. Tell them why you are so passionate about it and what makes it special to you. Ask them to do the same with a work of art they love.

3

CREATIVITY: MY THANKFUL THOUGHTS

Date:

Date:

CREATIVITY: MY THANKFUL THOUGHTS

Date: _____

Date:

"**Do all the good you can,
by all the means you can,
in all the ways you can,
in all the places you can,
at all the times you can,
to all the people you can,
as long as ever you can.**"

– Unknown (often attributed to John Wesley)

CHAPTER 4

gen•er•os•i•ty:

the quality of being kind, understanding and not selfish; the quality of freely giving or sharing money and other valuable things; the quality of showing kindness and concern for others

The Tire Iron and the Tamale

by Justin Horner

During this past year I've had three instances of car trouble: a blowout on the freeway, a bunch of blown fuses and an out-of-gas situation. They all happened while I was driving other people's cars, which made it even worse since I carry things like a jack and extra fuses in my own car.

Each time these things happened, I was disgusted with the way people didn't bother to help. I was stuck hoping my friends' roadside service would show, just watching tow trucks cruise past me. People at a gas station told me that they couldn't lend me a gas can "for safety reasons."

But you know who came to my rescue all three times? Immigrants. Mexican immigrants. None of them spoke any English.

One stopped to help me with the blowout even though he had his whole family of four in tow. I had been on the side of the road for close to three hours with my friend's Jeep®. I'd put big signs in the windows that said, "Need a jack" and offered money. Nothing. Right as I was about to give up and start hitching, a van pulled over, and a guy bounded out.

He sized up the situation and called for his daughter, who spoke English. He conveyed through her that he had a jack but that it was too small for the Jeep, so we would need to brace it. Then he got a saw from the van and cut a section out of a big log on the side of the road. We rolled it over, put his jack on top and we were in business.

I started taking the wheel off, and then, if you can believe it, I broke his tire iron. It was one of those collapsible ones, and I wasn't careful, and I snapped the head clean off.

No worries: He ran to the van and handed it to his wife, and she was gone in a flash down the road to buy a new one. She was back in 15 minutes. We finished the job with a little sweat and cussing, and I was a very happy man.

The two of us were filthy. His wife produced a large water jug for us to wash our hands with. I tried to put a $20 bill in the man's hand, but he wouldn't take it, so instead I went up to the van and gave it to his wife as quietly as I could. I thanked them up one side and down the other. I asked the little girl where they lived, thinking maybe I'd send them a gift for being so awesome. She said they lived in Mexico. They were in Oregon so Mommy and Daddy could pick cherries for the next few weeks, then peaches, then go back home.

After I said my goodbyes and started walking back to the Jeep, the girl called out and asked if I'd had lunch. When I told her no, she ran up and handed me a tamale.

I thanked them again and as I walked back to the car, I opened the foil on the tamale. What did I find inside? My $20 bill! I whirled around and ran back to the van. The guy saw the bill in my hand and just started shaking his head no. All I could think to say was, "Por favor, por favor, por favor," with my hands out. The guy just smiled and, with what looked like great concentration, said in English:

"Today you, tomorrow me."

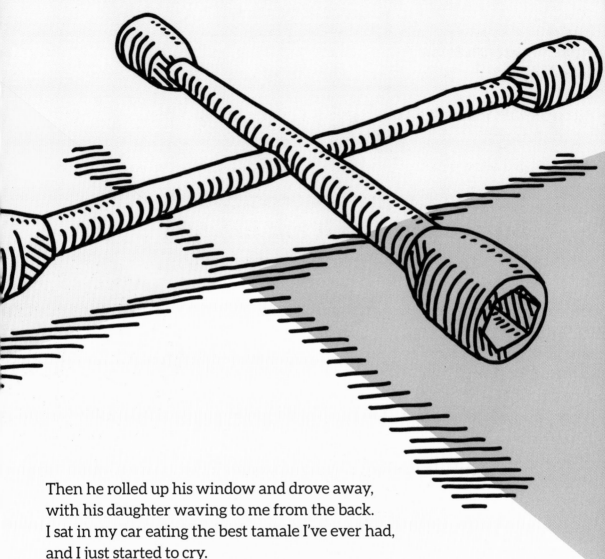

Then he rolled up his window and drove away,
with his daughter waving to me from the back.
I sat in my car eating the best tamale I've ever had,
and I just started to cry.

This family, undoubtedly poorer than just about everyone
else on that stretch of highway, working on a seasonal basis
where time is money, took a couple of hours out of their day
to help a strange guy on the side of the road while people in
tow trucks were just passing him by.

Since then I've changed a couple of tires, given a few rides to gas
stations and once drove 50 miles out of my way to get a girl to an airport.
I won't accept money. But every time I'm able to help, I feel as if I'm putting
something in the bank.

1

Reflect on the generosity of others and how it has brought you personal joy or inspiration.

What is the best gift you ever received that came in a package? Who gave it to you and for what occasion? What made it so special?

Do the same exercise with the best gift you ever received that *didn't* come in a package – advice, encouragement, wisdom, care or simply time spent together.

Take the time to sit down and thoughtfully and thoroughly consider what you have to give.

2

Focus on what you are able to do, and try not to let your thoughts drift to things that you are unable to do. You can be "wealthy" or "generous" in more ways than financially. Think about what you have to give physically – strength, energy, skill, intelligence or talent. Then think about what you have to offer from your heart – things like time, patience, advice or tolerance. Often people don't need money or material things, but they crave someone to listen generously to their soul. If you are having trouble thinking of what you have to give, ask a friend or family member to help. They may recognize gifts you may not even know you have.

Are you surprised at just how much you have to contribute to the good of your fellow human beings? Consider what a gift it is to have so much to give.

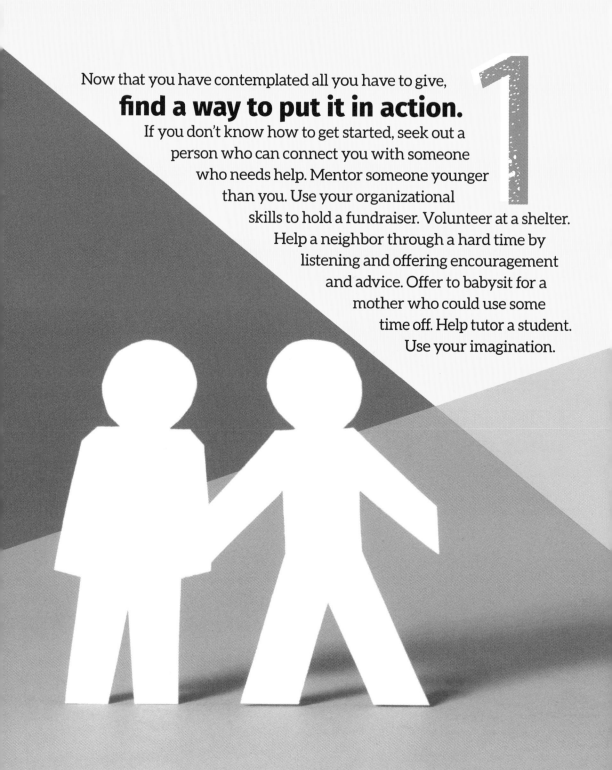

Now that you have contemplated all you have to give, **find a way to put it in action.** If you don't know how to get started, seek out a person who can connect you with someone who needs help. Mentor someone younger than you. Use your organizational skills to hold a fundraiser. Volunteer at a shelter. Help a neighbor through a hard time by listening and offering encouragement and advice. Offer to babysit for a mother who could use some time off. Help tutor a student. Use your imagination.

1

Commit yourself to actively contributing to a positive and generous environment.

Say hello, smile and wish people well. Hold the elevator for them. Compliment them on their clothing. Let them in front of you in line. Help put a positive spin on frustrations they might be experiencing.

While these may all seem like common pleasantries that don't amount to much, they are actually very powerful in gradually building a supportive environment and making people feel more open and caring. Do or say something kind to everyone you encounter.

2

GENEROSITY: MY THANKFUL THOUGHTS

Date: _____

Date: _____

GENEROSITY: MY THANKFUL THOUGHTS

Date:

Date:

"I AM STRUCK BY HOW SHARING OUR WEAKNESS AND DIFFICULTIES IS MORE NOURISHING TO OTHERS THAN SHARING OUR QUALITIES AND SUCCESSES."

– JEAN VANIER

CHAPTER 5

com•mu•ni•ty:

a group of people who live in the same area;
a group of people who have the same interests,
religion, race, etc.; social activity, fellowship

Why does social connection make us happy?

People are happier when they are with other people than when they are alone. You may not need a scientist or a researcher to tell *you* that – but lots of them have been delving into the reasons *why* close, caring relationships are so vital to our well-being and happiness. Here's what they've been learning.

Relationships give us mental space and feelings of **security**. When we know we are safe and supported, we can relax, explore, learn and grow because we don't have to fully dedicate our energy to basic survival or responding to danger. It also helps us develop resources for times of stress and hardship.

Relationships are good for our **health**. Those with strong social connections have fewer stress-related health problems, lower risk of depression and faster recovery from trauma. Friends and family can also encourage us to maintain healthy lifestyle habits, such as exercise and moderation.

Relationships instill in us a sense of **belonging** and help us feel like we're part of something larger than ourselves – which in turn sets the stage for higher self-esteem and achievement.

Think about it: if happy people are more pleasant and sociable, and being around other people makes us feel happier, then that makes us more fun to be around, too – creating an "upward spiral" of happiness!

Think about the different types of communities you belong to

– where you live, your place of worship, those who share your cultural identity or a club with a common interest. The next time you gather, relish the sights, sounds and smells you associate with each group – the aroma of hot coffee as you gather with neighbors for breakfast, someone's loud and distinctive laugh, or watching children play. Recognize the comfort and energy these sensory experiences bring you.

Consider how you feel and behave differently when you are by yourself instead of being among others. Do you carry yourself in another way? Do you wear different clothes? Do you smile less? Most important, how do your thoughts vary when you are alone? Do you worry more and focus too much on your own problems? Be aware of the physical and mental changes that happen when you are around others.

2

What have you learned about yourself from being part of a community?

3

What responsibilities and expectations do you have? How does it make you feel to contribute and participate?

Sharing stories is a practice that goes back to the earliest civilizations – keep it going!

Sit around the table with people and tell each other your best stories –

1

Your first car, your first scar or how you met the love of your life. Listen actively and try to remember many as you can. Later, write down the best one you heard.

Photo courtesy of the Girl Scouts of the United States of America. The image is from the 1954 Girls Scouts of the United States of America Girl Scout Calendar for the month of August, 1954.

Create the opportunity for someone else to experience the joy of community.

Invite them to a group event or volunteer effort. Be sure to let them know that you will appreciate their company as much as they would benefit from joining you. If they can't come to you, gather a group of people and go to them. Go out of your way to break the ice with some fun questions or activities and really make them feel welcome.

2

COMMUNITY: MY THANKFUL THOUGHTS

Date: _____

_____

_____

_____

_____

_____

_____

_____

_____

_____

_____

_____

_____

_____

_____

_____

_____

_____

_____

_____

_____

_____

Date: _____

COMMUNITY: MY THANKFUL THOUGHTS

Date: ....

> "As I walked out the door toward the gate that would lead to my freedom, I knew if I didn't leave my bitterness and hatred behind, I'd still be in prison."

– Nelson Mandela

CHAPTER **6**

for•give•ness:

the act of stopping feelings
of anger toward or blaming
someone who has done
something wrong; the act
of giving up resentment of
or claim to requital for

It would be easy – expected, even – for Mary Johnson and Oshea Israel to be enemies.

After all, he killed Johnson's only son, in 1993. He went to prison for that – and toward the end of his sentence, he and Johnson made peace.

As a teenager in Minneapolis, Israel was involved with gangs and drugs. One night at a party, he got into a fight with Laramiun Byrd, 20, and shot and killed him. Israel finished serving his prison sentence for murder in 2011.

The following is taken from a recorded conversation between Johnson and Israel in which they discuss their relationship and the forgiveness it is built upon.

As Johnson recalled, their first face-to-face conversation took place at Stillwater Prison, when Israel agreed to her repeated requests to see him.

"I wanted to know if you were in the same mindset of what I remembered from court, where I wanted to go over and hurt you," Johnson told Israel. "But you were not that 16-year-old. You were a grown man. I shared with you about my son."

"And he became human to me," Israel said.

At the end of their meeting at the prison, Johnson was overcome by emotion.

"The initial thing to do was just try and hold you up as best I can," Israel said, "just hug you like I would my own mother."

Johnson said, "After you left the room, I began to say, 'I just hugged the man that murdered my son.'

"And I instantly knew that all that anger and the animosity, all the stuff I had in my heart for 12 years for you – I knew it was over, that I had totally forgiven you."

Johnson founded *From Death to Life: Two Mothers Coming Together for Healing*, a support group for mothers who have lost their children to violence.

And for Israel, Johnson's forgiveness has brought both changes and challenges to his life.

"Sometimes I still don't know how to take it," he said, "because I haven't totally forgiven myself yet. It's something that I'm learning from you. I won't say that I have learned yet, because it's still a process that I'm going through."

"I treat you as I would treat my son," Johnson said. "And our relationship is beyond belief."

In fact, the two live right next door to one another in Minneapolis.

"So you can see what I'm doing – you know, firsthand," Israel said.

And if he falls out of touch, Israel is sure to hear about it from Johnson – who, Israel said, will call out to him, "'Boy, how come you ain't called over here to check on me in a couple of days? You ain't even asked me if I need my garbage to go out!'"

"Uh-huh," Johnson said with a laugh.

"I find those things funny, because it's a relationship with a mother for real," Israel said.

"Well, my natural son is no longer here. I didn't see him graduate. Now you're going to college. I'll have the opportunity to see you graduate," Johnson said. "I didn't see him getting married. Hopefully one day, I'll be able to experience that with you."

Hearing her say those things, Israel said, gives him a reason to reach his goals.

"It motivates me to make sure that I stay on the right path," he said. "You still believe in me. And the fact that you can do it, despite how much pain I caused you – it's amazing."

But Israel is not the only one who's impressed.

"I know it's not an easy thing, you know, to be able to share our story together," Johnson said. "Even with us sitting here looking at each other right now, I know it's not an easy thing. So I admire that you can do this."

"I love you, lady."

"I love you too, son."

Produced by Jasmyn Belcher Morris with the interview recorded by StoryCorps.

CONTEMPLATE IT

1

Think about the experience of being forgiven.

What difference has it made in how you live and how you feel? What possibilities has it opened for you?

2

Reflect on your experience with forgiving others.

Has it gotten easier or harder over the years? What has forgiving someone else taught you about yourself?

THINK OF SOMEONE YOU HAVE HAD A GRIEVANCE WITH AND HAVE SINCE FORGIVEN.

1

Did you simply forgive them in your own heart but not let them know directly? You might assume they know they are forgiven, or have forgotten about the subject altogether. The act of purposefully, clearly forgiving them will bring lightness to their heart and your own.

GIVE SOMEONE THE GIFT OF THE OPPORTUNITY TO FORGIVE YOU.

2

You are human! That means you have made a mistake or done something thoughtless at some point. It could be something big or small, just once or repeatedly over time. Is there something you regret? Is there a relationship that was important to you that is damaged or broken?

Write to that person. Explain what you are sorry for. Sincerely apologize. Then ask them to forgive you. Give them time to absorb and respond. Depending on the situation, it might not happen right away, or at all. The important thing is that you have opened up a possibility with nothing to lose and everything to gain.

If it feels good to forgive and good to be forgiven, then just imagine how exponentially incredible it will feel to FORGIVE YOURSELF.

3

Think of something you have never forgiven yourself for, even if someone else has already forgiven you for it. Try to remember all the circumstances and details around why you might have done what you did. Now look in the mirror and say out loud,

"I forgive you."

It's important to hear yourself say it – if it feels uncomfortable at first, you're doing it right. Say it again and as many times as you need to before you really feel it.

FORGIVENESS: MY THANKFUL THOUGHTS

Date: _____

_____

_____

_____

_____

_____

_____

_____

_____

_____

_____

_____

_____

_____

_____

_____

_____

_____

_____

_____

_____

_____

_____

_____

_____

_____

Date: _____

FORGIVENESS: MY THANKFUL THOUGHTS

Date: _____

Date: _____

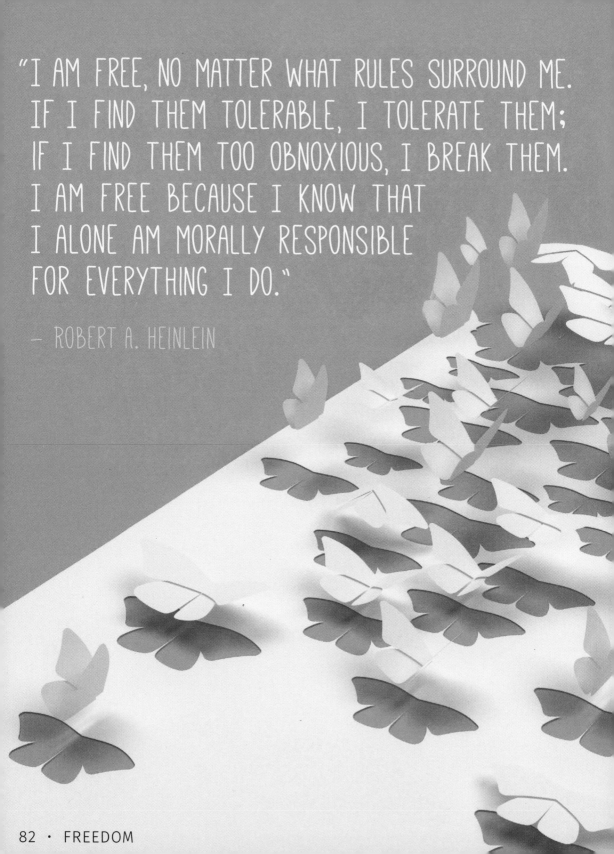

"I AM FREE, NO MATTER WHAT RULES SURROUND ME. IF I FIND THEM TOLERABLE, I TOLERATE THEM; IF I FIND THEM TOO OBNOXIOUS, I BREAK THEM. I AM FREE BECAUSE I KNOW THAT I ALONE AM MORALLY RESPONSIBLE FOR EVERYTHING I DO."

— ROBERT A. HEINLEIN

CHAPTER 7

free•dom:

the quality or state of being free;
the absence of necessity, coercion
or constraint in choice or action;
liberation from slavery or restraint or
from the power of another; independence

FREEDOM in old age is freedom to gather everything I have learned up to this point and to put it to even more exciting use now. It is the freedom to give myself away to those who really need me, in ways I have never had the chance of doing before. I am free to be important to people with real needs. And with that new role in life, I become one of those rare people who know what it takes to go through life, survive its dislocations, outlive its expectations, and negotiate its shoals. Now I am free to do it not simply for my own sake – but for the sake of the world at large.

When I realize that freedom really is the right to be me, rather than someone else – perhaps for the first time in my life – the liberation of the soul begins. And with it the unshackling of the mind. I can become something new, as well as simply more of the old. Because whatever path it was that got me here is not the only path I have ever considered, ever been fascinated by, ever wanted to explore.

So, why not now, when the exploration is boundaried by both common sense and a lifetime of experience?

I have the right now to explore new ideas, to think new thoughts. The ones I did not learn at home, the ones I have never dared to admit to in public. My answers will surely be as correct as anyone else's – and a great deal closer to my heart.

Finally, I am now free to become involved in life in ways I never did before when all the directions were clear and all the expectations binding and all the responsibilities defined.

A burden of these years is to allow all the stereotypes of old age to hold me back, to hold me down, to stop the flow of life in me.

A blessing of these years is that they give me the chance to break the bounds of a past life, and to create for myself a life more suited to what I now want to be.

– Sister Joan Chittister

Excerpt from the book *THE GIFT OF YEARS: Growing Older Gracefully* by Joan Chittister, reprinted by permission of BlueBridge/ United Tribes Media Inc.

Think back to the first time in your life you remember feeling free.

Those precious midair moments clinging to a rope before splashing down in the water. Getting behind the wheel with your brand-new driver's license. Finally mustering up the courage to put a bad relationship behind you and move on. Try to remember the experience in as much detail as you can. What was the first thing you did differently with your newfound freedom? What did you learn about yourself?

CONTEMPLATE IT

Intentionally consider how the specific freedoms we enjoy affect the simple activities of your everyday life. As you read the morning newspaper, appreciate our freedom of the press. If you attend a worship service, be grateful for our freedom of religion.

What would your life be like without these fundamental freedoms?

1 With the opening story of this chapter in mind, think about freedoms you enjoy today you may not have had when you were younger. Freedom to speak your mind with confidence. Freedom from responsibilities. Freedom to explore new ideas and interests.

Write an inspirational message to encourage yourself to take full advantage of your freedom –

for your personal growth and for the benefit of others.

FREEDOM MISSION STATEMENT

Fully participate in the processes of freedom and help preserve it for others.

2

Vote. Work at the polls or volunteer for a campaign you support. Share your perspective about freedom with a group of younger people and encourage them to get involved.

Acknowledge those who have served to protect our freedom.

3

Write a thank-you note to a soldier or a veteran, or perform an act of kindness when you see them – buy them lunch or a cup of coffee, have a conversation, or simply shake their hand and offer your sincere gratitude.

FREEDOM: MY THANKFUL THOUGHTS

Date: _____

Date:

FREEDOM: MY THANKFUL THOUGHTS

Date: _____

Date: _____

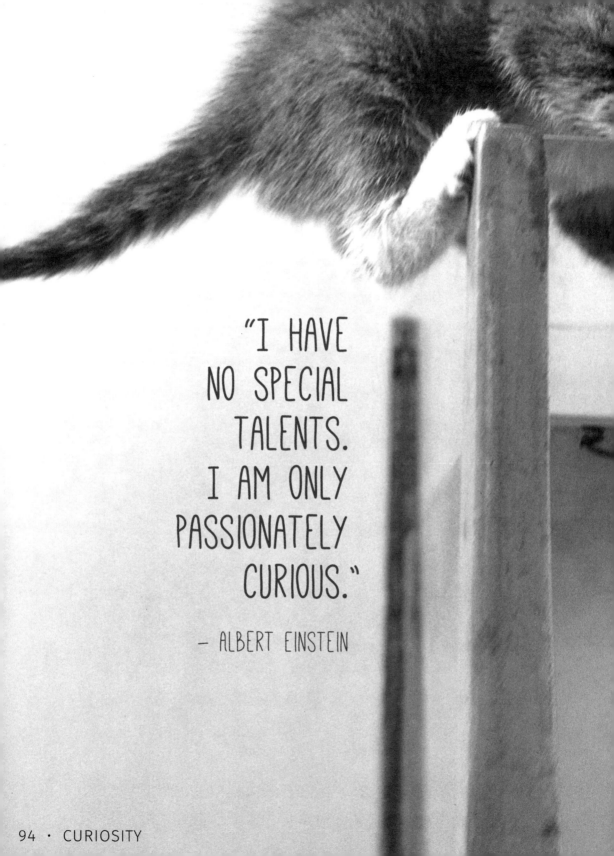

"I HAVE
NO SPECIAL
TALENTS.
I AM ONLY
PASSIONATELY
CURIOUS."

– ALBERT EINSTEIN

CHAPTER **8**

cu•ri•os•i•ty:

the desire to learn or know more
about something or someone;
interest leading to inquiry

Nuclear physicist Isidor Isaac Rabi,
winner of the Nobel Prize in physics in 1944,
was once asked why he became a scientist.

"My mother made me become a scientist
without ever intending to," he said. "Every other Jewish
mother in Brooklyn asked her child after school,
'So, did you learn anything today?'
But not my mother. 'Izzy,' she would say,

'DID YOU ASK A GOOD QUESTION TODAY?'

That difference – asking good questions –
made me become a scientist."

Sharing your *wonder* with younger generations
is just as important as sharing your *wisdom*.

Make observations about your surroundings.
Show that at any age, it's fun to ask questions,
discuss ideas and discover solutions together.
Like Rabi's mother, we can encourage
children to be curious.

CONSIDER HOW CURIOSITY HAS SHAPED AND DRIVEN YOUR LIFE FROM THE VERY BEGINNING.

1

Taking your first steps as a baby. Testing just how fast your new bike could go. Traveling to see how people live in other places. Whether you experienced pleasure or pain as a result, how would your life be different today if you hadn't tried? Has your level of curiosity changed over the years? If so, why? Be curious about your own curiosity.

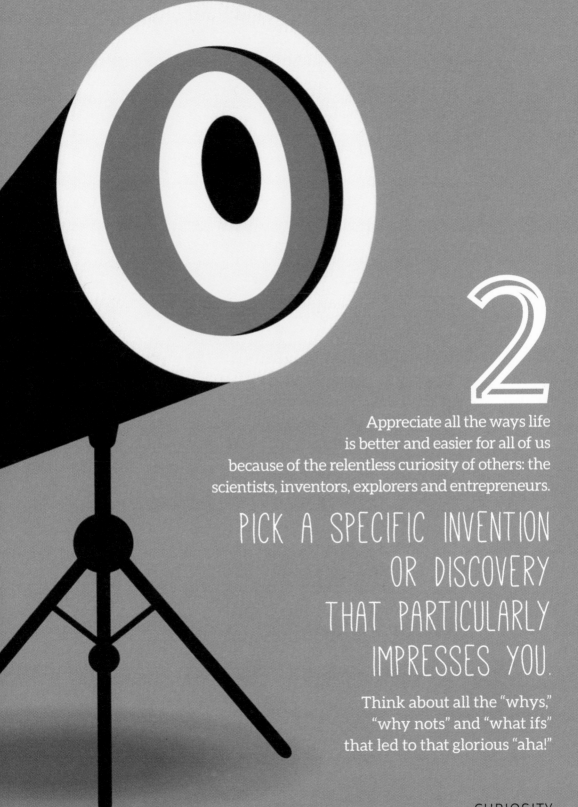

2

Appreciate all the ways life is better and easier for all of us because of the relentless curiosity of others: the scientists, inventors, explorers and entrepreneurs.

PICK A SPECIFIC INVENTION OR DISCOVERY THAT PARTICULARLY IMPRESSES YOU.

Think about all the "whys," "why nots" and "what ifs" that led to that glorious "aha!"

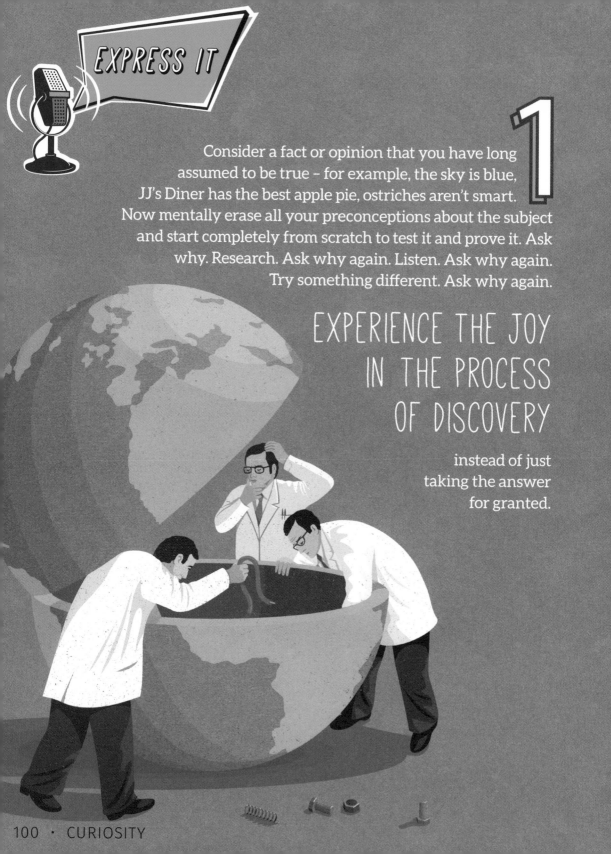

1

Consider a fact or opinion that you have long assumed to be true – for example, the sky is blue, JJ's Diner has the best apple pie, ostriches aren't smart. Now mentally erase all your preconceptions about the subject and start completely from scratch to test it and prove it. Ask why. Research. Ask why again. Listen. Ask why again. Try something different. Ask why again.

EXPERIENCE THE JOY IN THE PROCESS OF DISCOVERY

instead of just taking the answer for granted.

2

CALL OR WRITE A THANK-YOU NOTE TO SOMEONE WHO INDULGED AND NURTURED YOUR CURIOSITY

– a parent, a teacher, a caregiver, a neighbor or a friend. If the person has passed away, write a thoughtful testament about what they did and how it made a difference in your life, then share it with those who would appreciate it – their family, colleagues, neighbors or members of their church or synagogue.

3

CONSCIOUSLY INDULGE YOUR CURIOSITY.

Listen to a record you never in a million years think you will like. Attend the service of a different faith. Try something to eat you've never tried before (or didn't like the first time you tried it). Ask questions about anything and everything – even if it drives people crazy.

CURIOSITY: MY THANKFUL THOUGHTS

Date: _____

_____

_____

_____

_____

_____

_____

_____

_____

_____

_____

_____

_____

_____

_____

_____

_____

_____

_____

Date: _____

CURIOSITY: MY THANKFUL THOUGHTS

Date: _____

Date:

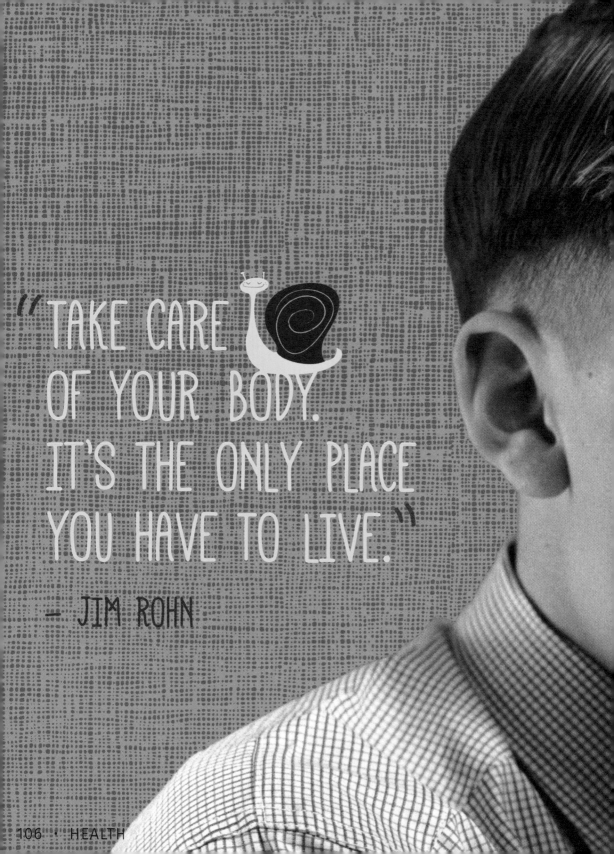

"TAKE CARE OF YOUR BODY. IT'S THE ONLY PLACE YOU HAVE TO LIVE."

– JIM ROHN

health:

the condition of being sound in body, mind or spirit; freedom from disease or pain; the overall condition of someone's body or mind; well-being

BEHOLD YOUR HUMAN BODY.

- Each day, your heart creates enough energy to drive a truck 20 miles (32 kilometers).

- When you are awake, your brain produces enough electricity to power a small lightbulb.

- Your nose can remember 50,000 different scents.

- Your eyes can distinguish almost 10 million different colors.

- Your heartbeat can follow and mimic the music you listen to.

- Nerve signals travel to and from your brain at up to 170 miles per hour (274 kilometers per hour).

- Ounce for ounce, your bones are stronger than steel.

- You use 200 muscles to take one step.

- When you wake up, you are about one centimeter taller than when you go to bed.

- About half of your hand strength is in your pinkie finger.

You are living in this incredibly intricate and powerful machine every day. Pardon it for the occasional technical difficulties, and reward it for all the remarkable things it does by feeding it well and keeping it moving.

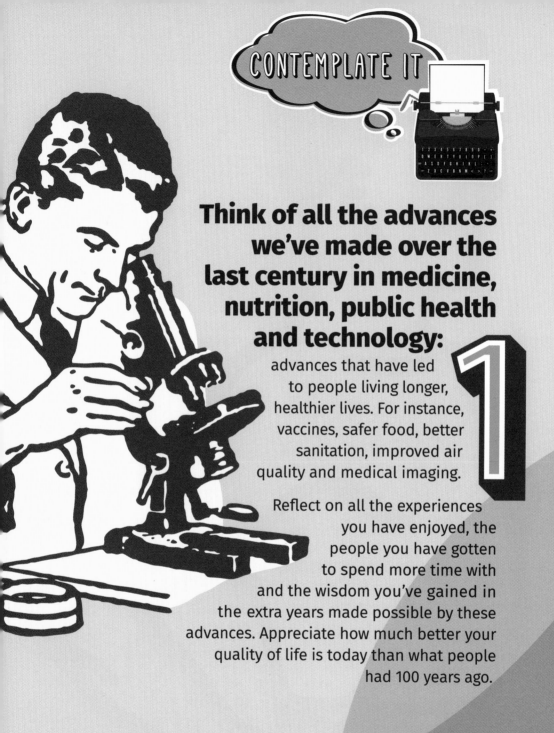

Think of all the advances we've made over the last century in medicine, nutrition, public health and technology: advances that have led to people living longer, healthier lives. For instance, vaccines, safer food, better sanitation, improved air quality and medical imaging.

Reflect on all the experiences you have enjoyed, the people you have gotten to spend more time with and the wisdom you've gained in the extra years made possible by these advances. Appreciate how much better your quality of life is today than what people had 100 years ago.

Do three simple things to nurture your health today.

2

Take a walk.
Eat a piece of fruit.
Spend time with
people you like.

As you do each, be conscious of all the details of how each is
nourishing your body. With each step, consider every muscle you're
moving, picture your heart pumping faster and growing stronger and
visualize the oxygen going in and out of your lungs. With each bite,
think of the nutrients and calories being digested and the vitamins
and minerals being distributed to your organs and muscles. As you listen
to and talk with others, be aware of your endorphin levels increasing.

Recognize the complex ways that simple, enjoyable actions

1

Make a list of every single positive aspect of your health you can think of.

For example, "I am optimistic. I have energy. I eat my vegetables. My blood pressure is under control. My teeth are strong. I'm at a healthy weight."

Be sure to include all the ways that you are healthy besides physically – emotionally, mentally and spiritually. By focusing on our healthiest traits rather than our weaknesses, we can better appreciate the total picture of our health.

Identify someone you know who has a positive effect on your health

– your exercise buddy, your caregiver, a chef who makes healthy food taste good, your grandchildren, your yoga instructor, your doctor or the produce manager at your local grocery. Write a note thanking them for all the ways they help you stay healthy.

2

HEALTH: MY THANKFUL THOUGHTS

Date: _____

_____
_____
_____
_____
_____
_____
_____
_____
_____
_____
_____
_____
_____
_____
_____
_____
_____
_____
_____
_____
_____
_____

Date: _____

HEALTH: MY THANKFUL THOUGHTS

Date: _____

Date: _____

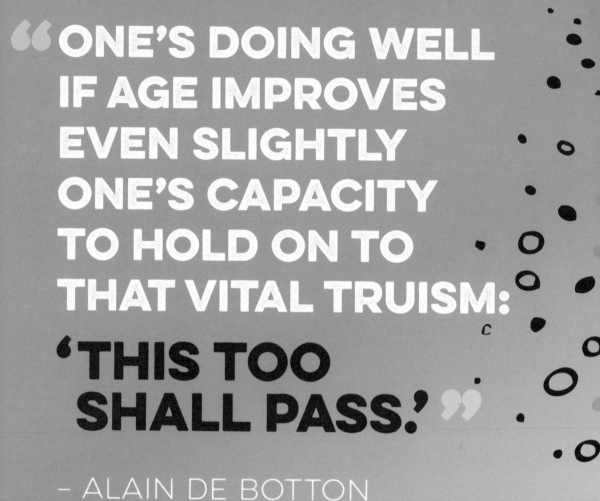

"ONE'S DOING WELL IF AGE IMPROVES EVEN SLIGHTLY ONE'S CAPACITY TO HOLD ON TO THAT VITAL TRUISM: 'THIS TOO SHALL PASS.'"

– ALAIN DE BOTTON

CHAPTER 10

re·sil·ience:
the ability to become strong, healthy or
successful again after something bad happens;
an ability to recover from or adjust easily

Some of the world's greatest success stories

- **Winston Churchill** failed the sixth grade and was defeated in every public office election he ran in before becoming British Prime Minister at age 65.

- **Thomas Edison** created 1,000 different lightbulbs before inventing one that worked.

- **Steven Spielberg** was rejected from his dream film school, the University of Southern California School of Cinematic Arts, twice.

- **Marilyn Monroe's** first contract with Columbia Pictures® expired because they told her she wasn't pretty or talented enough to be an actress.

- A newspaper editor fired **Walt Disney** because he "lacked imagination and had no good ideas."

- **Albert Einstein** didn't speak until age four and didn't read until age seven. His teachers labeled him "slow" and "mentally handicapped."

- In **Fred Astaire's** first screen test, the testing directors wrote: "Can't act. Can't sing. Slightly bald. Can dance a little."

- After **Sidney Poitier's** first audition, the casting director instructed him to stop wasting everyone's time and "go be a dishwasher or something."

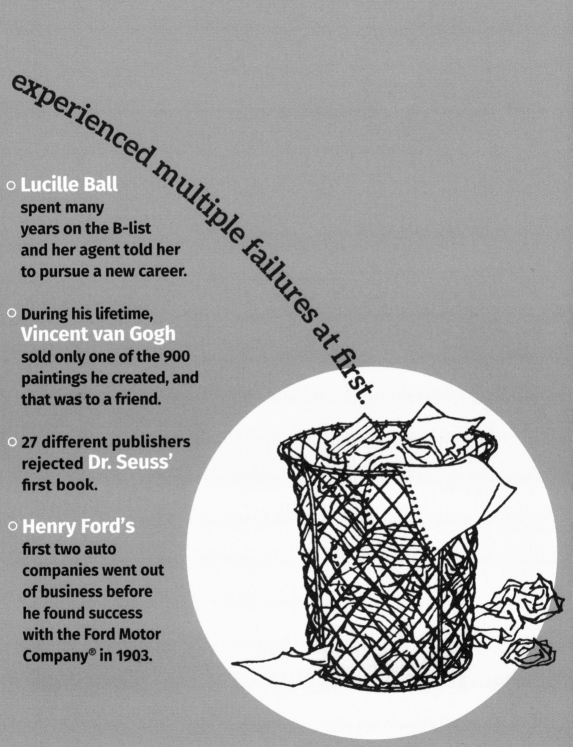

experienced multiple failures at first.

○ **Lucille Ball** spent many years on the B-list and her agent told her to pursue a new career.

○ During his lifetime, **Vincent van Gogh** sold only one of the 900 paintings he created, and that was to a friend.

○ 27 different publishers rejected **Dr. Seuss'** first book.

○ **Henry Ford's** first two auto companies went out of business before he found success with the Ford Motor Company® in 1903.

1

Picture yourself on a trampoline. You take your first jump and up you go. It's great up there! Coming back down is scary, but the next bounce propels you higher than before. And the next trip back down isn't as scary when you know you've bounced back before and will again, soaring higher still.

Appreciate every setback, every failure and every hardship you've had in your life.

They are the trips back down that lead to the bounces – your jumps wouldn't get stronger without them, and they help you reach greater heights of strength and happiness.

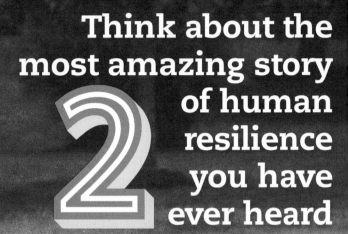

Think about the most amazing story **2** of human resilience you have ever heard

– someone who has faced unbelievable hurdles, overcome hopeless odds and endured unspeakable atrocities, only to come out the other side stronger and with newfound purpose.

How does it make you feel? That if they could do it, so could you? Do your own challenges seem small in comparison?

Recognize the gift of their story for the insight and inspiration it has given you.

1 Write a personal "comeback story"

based on a challenge or crisis you have overcome in your life. Focus on the specific ways you coped and discuss if there was a turning point where new possibilities opened up and you found unexpected opportunities. Give recognition to those who were there for you and helped you through it all – people you knew personally, authors whose works gave you strength, singers whose songs comforted you.

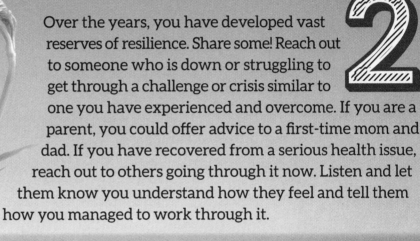

2

Over the years, you have developed vast reserves of resilience. Share some! Reach out to someone who is down or struggling to get through a challenge or crisis similar to one you have experienced and overcome. If you are a parent, you could offer advice to a first-time mom and dad. If you have recovered from a serious health issue, reach out to others going through it now. Listen and let them know you understand how they feel and tell them how you managed to work through it.

Be a living, breathing, inspiring personification of resilience.

RESILIENCE: MY THANKFUL THOUGHTS

Date:

RESILIENCE: MY THANKFUL THOUGHTS

Date: _____

Date: _____

RESILIENCE: MY THANKFUL THOUGHTS

Date: _____

Date: _____

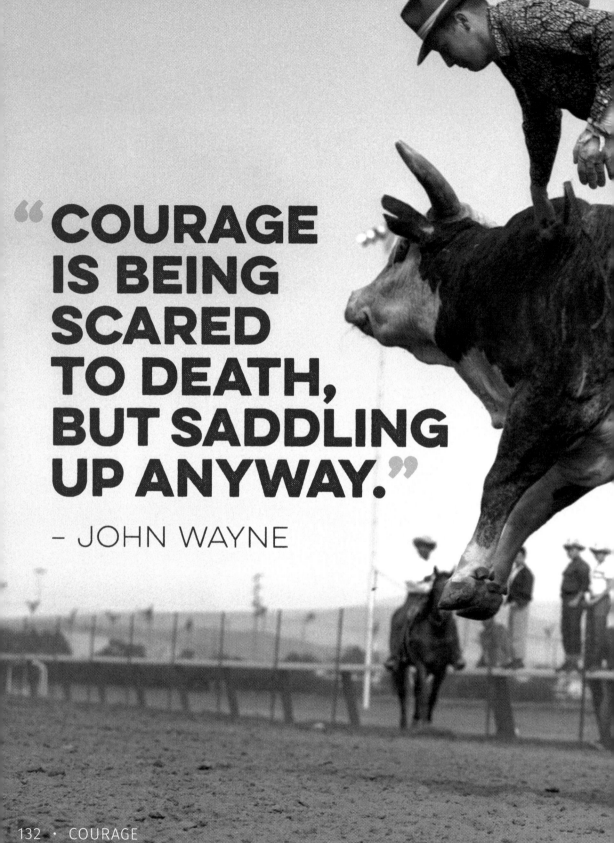

"COURAGE
IS BEING
SCARED
TO DEATH,
BUT SADDLING
UP ANYWAY."

– JOHN WAYNE

CHAPTER 11

cour•age:

the ability to do something
that frightens one; strength
in the face of pain or grief

The
Englishman
of Wenceslas Square

A few days before Christmas 1938, 29-year-old London stockbroker Nicholas Winton was packing for a ski holiday when he received a phone call that would change his life.

It was from his friend Martin Blake, a refugee assistance worker in Czechoslovakia, which was under threat from the Nazis. "I need your help with an assignment in Prague," he explained. "Don't bother bringing your skis."

Without hesitation, Winton boarded a train and checked into a hotel in Wenceslas Square. Blake then showed him the concentration camps where thousands of Jewish families were being forced to live in abhorrent conditions.

Realizing there was no specific plan in place to save the children – and failing to secure help from existing refugee organizations – Winton took it upon himself to cleverly create his own. He obtained stationery from the well-established British Committee for Refugees from Czechoslovakia and had printed beneath the heading: "Children's Section."

Winton then began collecting names. Word quickly spread of the "Englishman of Wenceslas Square," and parents began pleading with him to put their sons and daughters on his list. Three weeks later, he returned home to continue his work with the help of a few volunteers, including his own mother.

Over the course of nine months, Winton put 669 children on trains to London. Among them were Karel Reisz, who became a renowned author and film director; Joe Schlesinger, a journalist and author; and Renata Laxova, a pediatric geneticist.

Winton told no one of his deed for nearly 50 years, and his story did not become public until his wife, Grete, found a scrapbook in their attic containing lists of the names of the children, their parents and the families who took them in.

Even after being knighted in 2003, Winton continued to downplay his heroism, saying, "I just saw what was going on and did what I could to help." But his story illustrates how with courage, ordinary people can make extraordinary differences in the world.

In July 2015, Sir Nicholas Winton passed away at age 106 – 76 years to the day after many of the children he saved left Prague on a train to salvation.

COURAGEOUS
ACTS COME IN
MANY DIFFERENT
FORMS. SOMETIMES
THEY'RE SELFLESS
AND IMPACTFUL.
OTHER TIMES
THEY'RE LESS
EXTRAORDINARY,
LIKE FACING A
LONG-HELD PHOBIA.

ONE THING
ALL ACTS OF
COURAGE HAVE
IN COMMON
IS THEY INVOLVE
PUSHING PAST
FEAR TO
BETTER ONE'S
OWN — OR
SOMEONE ELSE'S —
CIRCUMSTANCES.

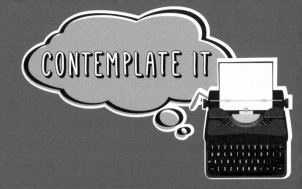

1

Think about the small ways you exhibit courage every day.

– trying a new food, introducing yourself to someone new or doing something by yourself for the first time. Make note of your little acts of courage today.

Now focus on 2 bigger acts of courage

you have performed throughout your life – times when fear was strong and stakes were high. For instance, pursuing a new career, starting a family, facing an illness or standing up for someone else in the face of adversity.

Thank yourself for the courage you've shown in life.

1
Remind yourself of the struggles you've overcome
– large and small – and recount out loud how you faced them.

2
Think about those who've shown courage on your behalf,
like family or first responders. List their names and the ways they affected your life. If you can, reach out to them; call or send a note letting them know how their courage made a difference in your life.

THIS IS FUN

A PUBLIC SERVICE

COURAGE: MY THANKFUL THOUGHTS

Date: _____

Date: _____

COURAGE: MY THANKFUL THOUGHTS

Date: _____

"The purpose of life is not to be happy – but to matter, to be productive, to be useful, to have it make some difference that you lived at all."

– Leo Rosten

pur•pose:

the reason for which something is done
or created, or for which something exists

Ikigai (**pronounced ee-ki-guy**) is the Japanese concept of *purpose*. Loosely translated, it means, **"the reason I get up in the morning."**

The concept is rooted in the belief that everyone has an ikigai, and finding it requires a deep and lengthy search of self. The search is highly regarded, as the discovery of one's ikigai is believed to bring satisfaction and meaning to life.

But there is another benefit to consider, too. Dr. Robert N. Butler – Pulitzer Prize-winning author, psychiatrist and expert on aging – led an 11-year study examining the correlation between one's sense of purpose and the length of one's life.

He followed healthy people between the ages of 65 and 92, and found those who expressed having clear goals or purpose lived longer and better than those who did not. He concluded this was because individuals who understood what brings them joy and happiness were more apt to participate in activities and be part of communities where they could immerse themselves in a rewarding and gratifying environment.

Not surprisingly, he found citizens of Okinawa, where the concept of ikigai is central to their culture, have a longer life expectancy than anyone else in the world.

Robert Butler later became a colleague, collaborator and friend of Atria, and his vision continues to inspire Atria's mission and programs. The Dr. Robert N. Butler Active Aging Center at Atria West 86 in Manhattan was created in his honor.

THAT
WHICH
THE
WORLD
NEEDS

THAT WHICH
YOU LOVE

MISSION

PASSION

THAT
WHICH
YOU ARE
GOOD
AT

IKIGAI

VOCATION

PROFESSION

THAT WHICH
YOU CAN BE PAID FOR

1

When you wake up tomorrow morning, be particularly aware of your very first thoughts. If they are filled with anxiety or dread, redirect them to positive ones. Promise yourself to do one thing that has the potential to bring you joy or a sense of accomplishment before you go to bed. Throughout the day, consider how each action you take – even if it isn't fun – contributes to your overall satisfaction.

Repeat each day and soon you will find yourself waking up in a more purposeful frame of mind.

It's just as important to help others live out their purpose as it is to live out your own.

When you need and accept someone's help, you are giving them the grace-filled gift of fulfilling their purpose. When you were a child, you helped your parents fulfill their purpose of raising and nurturing a family. These days, you may be offering a friend or caregiver the opportunity to fulfill their purpose of serving others.

2

Make a list of the people who made your life better in the process of living out *their* purpose. Make another list of people who have given you the opportunity to live out *your* purpose.

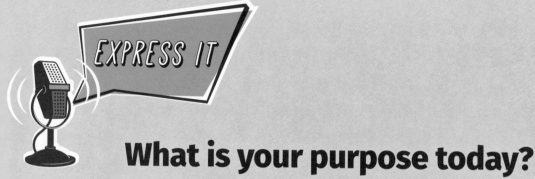

What is your purpose today?

A Declaration of Purpose is a way to focus your energy, actions, behaviors and decisions toward the things that are most important to you right now. The questions below are intended to help you clarify and identify your personal purpose.

So, let's get started! Answer the questions by yourself or team up with a friend. Either way, it's important to *write down your answers*. To avoid overthinking it, try and write the first thing that pops into your head, and give yourself less than a minute per question. Be honest. Try smiling as you write, as it will help keep your mind in an open place.

1. What are you naturally good at? Examples include skills, abilities and talents.

2. What activities make you lose track of time?

3. What were your favorite things to do when you were younger? What about now?

4. What are some things you want to do or appreciate more?

5. What are your three deepest values, in order of importance? Why are they important to you?

6. Who has been an influential person in your life or someone you admire?

7. If you had to teach something, what would it be?

8. What have been three of your biggest successes in life? These could be at work, in your community, at home, etc.

9. Where do you have the desire to make a difference? Examples include the world in general, your family, your friends and your community.

Now use your answers to create a declaration. Here are some templates you can use as seeds to start.

"To live each day with [one to three values or principles] so that [what living by these values will give you]. I will do this by [specific behaviors you will use to live by these values]."

"To treasure above all else [most important things to you] by [what you can do to live your priorities]."

"To be known by [a person/group] as someone who is [qualities you want to have]."

"To develop and cultivate the qualities of [two to three values/ character traits] that I admire in [an influential person in your life] so that [why you want to develop these qualities]."

Feel free to combine these sentences in any way to carve your own unique declaration. Here is an example:

"To develop and cultivate the qualities of creativity and expression that I admire in my granddaughter so that we can share the love of art and music together with the rest of the family."

Finally, remember that a Declaration of Purpose is not meant to be written once and etched in stone – you can change it or make a new one. But this exercise will allow you to have your purpose close to your heart today and to share it with others.

Congratulations on your Declaration of Purpose!

PURPOSE: MY THANKFUL THOUGHTS

Date: _____

Date:

PURPOSE: MY THANKFUL THOUGHTS

Date: _____

Date:

PURPOSE: MY THANKFUL THOUGHTS

Date: _____

Date: _____

Well done! You have learned how to make the gratitude in your heart a more powerful force in your life. You have become more present to all the goodness and wonder around you. And you have opened yourself to experiencing greater happiness and fulfillment.

That calls for a big

"THANK YOU, ME."

Imagine what it would be like if everyone lived in a constant state of gratitude. By setting an example with your actions and sharing the wisdom of gratitude with others, you are leaving a legacy that will make the world a better place for generations to come.

ACKNOWLEDGMENTS

STORY AND QUOTATION CREDITS

p. 32 Quote from the book
IGNORE EVERYBODY: AND 39 OTHER KEYS TO CREATIVITY
by Hugh MacLeod, copyright © 2009 by Hugh MacLeod,
used by permission of Portfolio, an imprint of
Penguin Publishing Group, a division of
Penguin Random House LLC.

IMAGE CREDITS

p. 62 Library of Congress, Prints & Photographs Division,
photograph by Harris & Ewing, LC-DIG-hec-23587

p. 84 Library of Congress, Prints & Photographs Division,
photograph by Harris & Ewing, LC-DIG-hec-23379

p. 160 Library of Congress, Prints & Photographs Division,
FSA/OWI Collection, LC-DIG-fsa-8d21674